T0198640

JUST *who* DO YOU THINK *you* ARE?

Identifying One's Personality in a World of Many

John Robbins

authorHOUSE®

AuthorHouse™
1663 Liberty Drive
Bloomington, IN 47403
www.authorhouse.com
Phone: 1 (800) 839-8640

Published by AuthorHouse 02/22/2018

ISBN: 978-1-5462-2528-7 (sc)
ISBN: 978-1-5462-2529-4 (hc)
ISBN: 978-1-5462-2530-0 (e)

Library of Congress Control Number: 2018900761

Print information available on the last page.

Any people depicted in stock imagery provided by Thinkstock are models, and such images are being used for illustrative purposes only. Certain stock imagery © Thinkstock.

This book is printed on acid-free paper.

ACKNOWLEDGMENTS

THIS BOOK WAS made possible by many friends and business acquaintances that have shared part of their lives with me. All of the traits that are included by no means are meant to degrade or misrepresent anyone. Please understand that these observations are strictly my own and may not be in agreement with every reader. Isn't it great that we all have our own opinion?

I received encouragement from family members and the **BAY**SOLUTIONS Team toward this Project. Thanks to Rachel Cline, Shay Catrett and Gail Robbins for their editing assistance. A very special thanks to Tiffany Dodson for the hours that she spent organizing and working on the books' layout.

ABOUT THE COVER

THE COVER OF this book was designed by JoBeth Robbins, a 5th grade school teacher. She teaches gifted students in Shelby County Alabama.

The silhouette of a head filled with chapter titles symbolizes the many personalities or traits that each of us as individuals possess.

CONTENTS

PREFACE: JUST WHO AM I?

◆

AS WE TRAVEL down the road of life, we get to meet and build relationships with all types of people. Some are very easy to get to know and simply a joy to be around; others may be more of a challenge and we find it difficult to get very close to them. Is it our fault, or theirs?

Many times, we don't stop to consider how others perceive us. We just trod along, living our lives, making some folks like us while others despise us. Have you ever considered how you stack up? Do others like you and want to spend as much time as possible with you? Or do they go out of their way to avoid being in your presence?

In this book, I identify many of the different personality traits of individuals which I have encountered in my life. Some characteristics stand alone, while other may overlap. Perhaps, you will find yourself in a number of these. I did!

It has often been said, "You must first identify the problem before you can go about solving it." As you read this book, try to pick out traits about yourself that you would like to modify or even eliminate. Keep in mind that you may also find traits that you want to improve or develop. It is hard to take an in-depth look at ourselves. Hopefully, this book will help you to do so and encourage you to make positive changes.

CHAPTER 1

RESUME BUILDERS

FROM TIME TO time, you run across individuals that volunteer to join every cause known to man. They enjoy having the title or reputation of being involved. Many times, the level of involvement is diminished by the mere volume of activities for which they have volunteered.

Peter Drucker was never more right than when he wrote "Concentration is the key to economic results...no other principal of effectiveness is violated as constantly as the basic principal of concentration. Our motto seems to be: Let's Do a Little Bit of Everything!"

This dilutes the efforts of everything that we do. Why do you think that medical practice is so specialized? Most brain surgeons can't perform hair transplants. Most plumbers can't do electrical work. Undertakers can't deliver babies. Simply, none of us can master every subject!

We need to seek out volunteer activities that have value; something that is interesting and in an area where we can contribute. Nothing upsets me more than to be on a board or committee with folks who don't carry their part of the load. They only want to add another line to their resume.

When someone asks you to do something, whether a favor or chore, ask yourself two questions: First, "Is it something I have to do?" And second, "Is it something I want to do?" You just might learn to say "no" more often. In the process, you'll begin to create more time for things that matter. And it may make you a happier and more genuine person because when you say "yes", it's less likely to be out of obligation.

It's important to remember that our lives are made up of 1,440 minutes each day. Our time is precious, and we can learn to treat it as such.

Bill Dresser, a Senior Manager for a telephone company I worked for, gave me a book many years ago while I was working my way through the Chairs of United Way. The book addressed the subject of volunteers that did not carry their load. It pointed out that such individuals should be removed from the team; basically, it was about the method to fire a volunteer. Team members that don't contribute cost others time and energy.

One of the things that we implemented on a number of boards on which I have served was an attendance page. If you missed two unexcused meetings within a twelve-month period, you were dropped from the board.

It is important that we learn to say "NO" when asked to participate in activities that will not add value to you personally or help promote your business. There will be plenty of other opportunities in the future. Don't be a resume builder!

As a small business owner, you are required to wear many hats. One of the most important is the hiring of you team. Most companies will advertise and review the resumes they receive before scheduling an interview. I have studied the value of a resume. It is interesting to notice thought-out my life, the changes that have been made regarding the information and format that is recommended to be used when preparing resumes.

Not so many years ago, a detailed history of all your accomplishments:

the more the better, were important. Today, it is recommended that the content be limited to one page.

Education, previous occupation, community involvement and your reason for wanting to work for the new Company is all that matters!

The most important factor is to be honest and sincere. Never present a false image.

CHAPTER 2

KNOW IT ALL'S

H AVE YOU EVER had a conversation with someone that would always do a "one-up" on you? In other words, no matter what subject that you brought up, they always knew more about it than you? Many times, they will make themselves the subject matter expert and try to convince you and those around of their superior knowledge.

A few years ago, such a person moved to our community. If you told a story about some experience that you had encountered, he would immediately answer with his own version of the same experience. He had flown all types of airplanes, caught every kind of fish, owned just about every type of automobile, dated more women and owned every kind of business that you could image.

One afternoon, a group of us gathered for a social meeting. We decided that we would play a game with our new friend. Each of us picked a topic that we would bring up at our meeting. One old timer said that he was going to talk about a tractor dealership of which he was once part owner. You guessed it, no sooner than the topic was brought up, the new comer began to tell us about a tractor dealership that he once owned.

It is not easy to relax and enjoy true fellowship with folks that always know more than you. Interestingly enough, if we are not careful, we can fall into the same trap. If we correct others when they are talking, we may be labeled with an "I know more than you" title. Often it is very difficult to refrain from correcting a statement that we know is incorrect. However, most of the time it is better to correct people in private and praise folks in public.

My wife has this art mastered. She is my greatest critic. She started early in our relationship. Many times, after we have been out for some special event, on the way home she will ask me a question regarding a topic that had been discussed earlier. Based on my response, she will tactfully share her knowledge of the subject. Most of the time, we both learned from these encounters.

It is not necessary to correct every mistake that we witness. Sometimes the difference is not worth the hassle. After all, each of us is entitled to our interpretation of life's experiences. I was in a class once when the instructor asked of us to write down the definition of chocolate. It was amazing as we each read our thoughts, how different our answers were. None were wrong in the mind of the writer. Some seemed to match closer with my thoughts. However, the point that was made is that we all perceive things a little differently. The question is, "Can we accept another's definition?" Or do we know it all?

CHAPTER 3

WANABES

I T HAS BEEN said that the greatest compliment is to be imitated. Athletes often mimic stars in their same profession. Entertainers will improvise a line from others. Many comics learn to follow the lead of others that have been successful. Some of the worlds' most renowned military leaders study the battle plans of others and develop similar plans.

I remember a story that my mother told about our first cousin Elton. He was the youngest grandchild of Grandma and Grandpa Straughn. He spent a lot of time with Grandpa because they lived close and they both idolized one another. Elton grew up talking and walking just like Grandpa. To this very day he sounds just like him.

Children often mock others and play mimicking activities that they see their parents or older siblings doing. This is natural and is part of growing up. As we grow up, the trap that a lot us fall into is that we become jealous of other folks' material things. As children we pointed out to our parents when begging for something: but so-in-so has one, or all my friends get too, why can't I?

It gets a lot worse when adults look at their neighbor or a friend and decide that they must have a new car, a new dress, or whatever else just to keep up with them. This can develop into a "want-to-be" syndrome which can lead to financial difficulties.

I have been guilty of telling older men of whom I respected and admired for their life successes, "When I grow up I want to be just like you!" Way down deep inside, I really would like to posses some of their traits. We all should look at successful folks and adopt some of their positive traits but not long for the material things just to keep up with our neighbors.

There is nothing wrong with learning from others. We just don't need to lose our own identity or become something that we are not. Remember, "Be what you is, 'cause if you is what you ain't, you ain't what you is." Not very good grammar, but you get the point!

I picked up this placard at a yard sale, framed it and placed it in a highly visible place in my office.

It is natural to pick out successful role models and pattern part of our daily activities that will help us to achieve as they have. As a very young man, growing up in small rural town, I began to dream of being a banker. My reason was that they seemed to always have money, nice cars, and big houses. This drove me to write to the United States Federal Reserve and request information about starting a bank. Little did I know that this desire would follow me for many years?

After completing a thirty-five-year career with the telephone company, together with several other investors, we created a new community bank. During the process, my mind drifted back to the things that I had read and dreamed about as a young lad.

There is truly only one man that we should all want to be like. His name was Jesus.

CHAPTER 4

HUMBLE AND UNDERCOVER

◆

ON OCCASION, MY wife Gail, her mother, and I travel to Troy, Alabama where we meet our son and his family. They drive down from their home in Birmingham. Usually we will meet at one of two places and have a leisurely lunch. This is quality time that we get to spend with our grandchildren. After lunch we will go shopping together or to a park where the kids can play after which we find a place to enjoy some ice cream.

On one of our trips, we met at the Ruby Tuesday restaurant. We arrived shortly before 11:00 A.M. which was opening time. However, the manager allowed us to enter and arranged several tables, thus allowing us all to be together. Mom's sisters joined us.

We all ordered our lunches and were served. The children waited until everyone had their order and then reached out to join hands. This is their tradition. The girls then sang the blessing for our meal prayer. This was followed by a short verbal prayer by my granddaughter Anna Grace. I was so proud of my family. As we finished, I noticed that both college students that were our servers had stopped what they were doing and bowed their heads.

After a wonderful meal followed by the dessert of our choice, I asked for the bill. The head waitress came over to me and said, "Your tab has been covered;" "By who?" I asked. Her answer was, "they didn't want you to know." On many occasions, I have quietly paid other folks' bills and left the restaurant without the recipient knowing, but it had never happened to me.

There are truly humble and caring folks in this world. We should all practice paying things forward. My mother was quick to share even when she had very little to give. She often told us that it is better to give than receive, however it should always be done with a humble and caring attitude. Never should it be done just to gain personal attention or to toot your own horn.

The next time that you drive through a toll booth, pay for the car behind you. Or purchase tickets to a special event that you know a friend would like to attend. Mail the tickets anonymously, and wait to witness their reaction. It is refreshing to do things for others without being identified. We can teach ourselves to be humble and not out front. When was the last time that you did such an act?

CHAPTER 5

NATURAL LEADERS

IT HAS BEEN said that you are either born with or without leadership skills. To some degree this is true. However, with the proper coaching and a genuine desire, these skills can be enhanced.

Some people project leadership simply by their stature, attractive looks, or verbal expressions. The best leaders listen more than they speak. It has been said, "Why did God give us two ears and only one mouth?" A good leader listens 80% of the time and talks only 20%.

I have trouble listening. Perhaps in today's busy environment there is so much noise that we have a tendency to block a lot out. When we do, we miss both the good and the bad.

Have you ever met a leader that did not care for their people or have a passion for their cause? Leaders set the example and never ask more than they give. In war, they are always on the front line. The best definition of leadership that I have read is: "The ability to get things done through others without creating hostility."

There is something about a natural leader that makes us want to follow. If you want to be a leader you can simply focus on the things that motivate you and why. Perhaps if we thought about the traits that we admire in folks who we consider to be leaders and developed the same skills, we too could become leaders! It is important that you feel the calling and do not create a false purpose. King Solomon asked for wisdom above all other gifts and we need to do the same.

We need to remember the greatest leader of all was a very low-profile individual that never tried to project a superior attitude. It may take a life time for others to truly understand the leader that you are. Hold yourself to your own high standards and you will always be a leader. A very important ingredient is love. Benjamin Franklin said, "If you would be loved, love and be lovable."

The older that I become, the easier it is for me to love others, even those that I didn't necessarily think much of in the past. We learn to forgive and forget. Small children love everyone. Perhaps, I am returning to my childhood. There is a special book that teaches us to love our neighbors as thy self.

The best leaders love their people. This creates the foundation to communicate and build trust. If you ever lose the trust of your people you will never regain it. A good leader leads by example. They don't ask anything from their team members that they themselves would not undertake. They always praise publicly and provide negative feedback privately.

CHAPTER 6

INAUTHENTIC

IT HAS BEEN said: If we could buy some people for what they are worth and sell them for what they think they are worth, then we would be rich. Have you ever wondered what causes people to try and be something other than themselves?

I have read that often folks with inferiority complexes subconsciously act differently than others. An example that comes to my mind is short men: They want to make up for their stature and do so by taking on a dictatorial style personality. Consider Napoleon Bonaparte. Standing at just 5' 6", the French military leader and emperor used his insight, ambition and skilled military strategy to conquer much of Europe in the early 19th century. What he lacked in height he made up in power and his legacy has made him one of the most celebrated and controversial political figures in human history.

Another life observation has pointed to individuals that grew up in a humble or very poor environment. Often, they want to exhibit any financial success openly, even to the point of exaggeration; "Look, I am rich…just what do you think about me?" Most of the time, folks with sound financial means are far more reserved. It is very difficult to become close to such people. You never know if you are dealing with the truth or some artificial and cosmetic statement. This seems to be the custom in today's politics.

It is normal for us from time to time to present ourselves in somewhat of an elevated posture. Some people do it under the influence of alcohol or drugs; others do it in a group setting where they can be the center of attention. Simply put, most of the time we do it in a normal day to day activity among our peers or family just to gain approval.

How we present ourselves determines how others perceive us. A gaudy or over-the-top appearance can drastically affect others' impressions of someone. The style of clothing or neatness of personal grooming plays such an important role.

My father, for example, did not own anything but long sleeve white shirts. He wore them to work as a salesman and to feed the chickens or work in the garden. He also wore a short-brimmed hat everywhere the year round. Often, he wore a tie. Most people that met him thought that he was a minister. He was a real southern gentleman with no money. Sometimes he would have some metal washers or other items that would make a clinging noise in his pocket. Perhaps he pretended that it was pocket change!

Through a life time of reading and studying, I have learned that it is healthy to dream about and act out successes that we want to achieve. It has been said that if you can dream it, you can accomplish it...the key is being authentic. The next time that you see someone that over dresses or wears too much jewelry, just observe them for a while. You may determine that they are trying to project a less than honest persona. What do others see in us?

CHAPTER 7

SOCIALITE

VERY CLOSELY RELATED to inauthentic is a socialite. Some of us are naturally sociable, but that doesn't make us a socialite. What, exactly, is the difference? A sociable person seems to fit in or enjoy crowds. Often, they exhibit a talent that allows them to communicate with complete strangers. They promote conversation by asking questions or complimenting others. They understand the protocol associated with the event and conduct themselves accordingly. This type of person could also be referred to as extroverted.

On the other hand, a socialite is someone that never wants to be left out of anything that can bring attention to themselves. They go out of the way to be involved in activities whether they are invited or not. It would destroy them to be involved in a conversation about any special event taking place within the community and not know all of the details.

Most socialites pride themselves at keeping up with the latest fashions, hair styles, and just about anything considered to be trendy. They never want to be the "out of date" person, regardless of the cost. Often, they are driven to buy the latest gadget and show it off. Sometimes, this causes financial burdens that can lead to bankruptcy.

A friend of mine once published a weekly newspaper that featured a very prominent neighborhood within our community. Most families that lived within the gated, upscale waterfront development were wealthy or at least wanted you to think so. My friend wrote about cars that were repossessed, utilities that were disconnected for non-payment and other financial problems that often led to broken homes and divorce. He enjoyed pointing out new jewelry, boats and cars that were bought by those that he knew couldn't afford them. His point was simple: Live within your means. Don't become such a socialite that it will cost you everything!

CHAPTER 8

RELIGIOUS

—————◆—————

OUR PARENTS TAUGHT us to judge not, less you be judged. It bothers me when so-called religious people start telling you all about your short comings. There is a story in the Bible that teaches us about letting those without guilt cast the first stone. It was intended to make us stop and look at ourselves before we judge others.

Throughout my life, I have been blessed by having known really good people. I have found that individuals who were the most religious were humble and always giving without expecting a return or recognition. Often, they refuse to see the bad in others and when they do, they find positive methods to help. They practice the Dale Carnegie rule, DO NOT CONDEMN, CRITICIZE, OR COMPLAIN. My mother would tell us, if we could not say something good about someone, don't say anything at all.

Some people like to wear their religion on their sleeve. They always want to be the person to say a prayer publicly and love it when they are named the Chaplin of any club or organization. They exhibit bumper stickers on their cars that indicate they are Christians and often wear bold crosses to magnify their thoughts about themselves. We need to be very careful how we boast about how perfect we think we are!

One of the best friends in my life was Brother Si Matheson. He was called to preach in the middle of his life. He came from a small North Florida town. He studied and became an ordained Methodist minister. Brother Si preached in a variety of churches throughout our area: small, large, white, black, and non-denominational. In my mind, he exhibited the spirit of Jesus in that he did not discriminate against anyone.

Curtis, a close friend of mine that passed away several years ago, had a special meaning of religion. His thoughts dealt more along the lines of the Native Americans. He loved and respected the outdoors, and any part of nature was special to him. He hunted and fished and was best known for his skills at harvesting wild turkey.

Many late afternoons, Curtis and I would ride in his pickup truck to one of the hunting leases to which he belonged. After unlocking the gates and entering hunter's paradise, Curtis would drive about 5 miles per hour. He would stop often, get out of the truck, and examine deer, turkey, and other wildlife tracks. He also looked at the grass, plants, and trees for signs that some of God's creatures had passed along the way.

He would be very quiet…almost as if in Church. Often, he would whisper to me to listen for natures' sounds. Many times, he would say to me, "This is about as close to God that anyone alive can possibly get."

Any type of religion should be respected if the individual practicing their belief is honest and sincere in their efforts. However, no one has the right to force their doctrine on someone else.

CHAPTER 9

FUN TO BE AROUND

------◆------

ARE YOU ONE of those people that draw others to you? Do you have magnetic charisma and the personality that makes you easy to like? Attitude is the key to being a positive person. We all enjoy the company of happy, honest, and healthy people. Generally, they talk and act in a manner that make us feel good. It has been said, "Attitudes are contagious, is yours worth catching?"

We all have our good and bad days. However, those with the greatest resistance to stress seem to have more control over their emotional swings. Have you ever been told that you are always upbeat and happy, no matter the daily challenges? We may not have control of what happens to us, but we can learn to be in charge of how we respond and act. We need to think positive thoughts, read positive books, and genuinely concentrate on subjects that we like.

Try this challenge. Start each day by finding something new for which you should be thankful. It may be as simple as a bird singing or a beautiful sunrise. Think about the joy that life's little things bring. Next find someone to compliment. It could be the paper boy or the lady where you buy your morning coffee. Say what comes easy but do it from your heart. If you read the morning newspaper, don't put it down until you find something that makes you count your blessings. At work, when that first telephone call comes in, put a smile in your voice and be thankful that you can hear the other party no matter what their message might bring.

Then as you move through the day, take extra care to go out of your way to make those around you feel good. Do not criticize, condemn, or complain. Find the good in everything and after a while, it will make you the person who is fun to be around.

Positive reinforcement propels us all to move forward. Our children need it, our workforce needs it, our bosses need it and yes, we need it. It has often been said, "We get out of life, what we put into it." Since everyone needs words of encouragement, it is to our advantage to practice giving others positive reinforcement because we will reap what we sow, and it will help us be fun to be around.

CHAPTER 10

SYMPATHY SEEKERS

❖

HAVE YOU EVER meet a person that thrived on sympathy? Our father, as great as he was, had an unusual characteristic. Any time a member of the family became ill, he suddenly had a more severe case of whatever they had. It was a way of drawing attention to himself. It was as if he was pleading, "Please feel sorry for me!"

My granddaughters like to pull the symphony trick to gain attention or get approval for something that they want. Perhaps it is somewhat natural for us all on occasion to feel sorry for ourselves and reach out for someone to provide that motherly touch. Even my little dog has learned how to demand special attention. She will lie down at your feet and wait to be picked up and loved.

Such action is often noticed in the behavioral patterns of homeless people that are looking for a handout and not a hand up. It reminds me of the man standing beside the road with a sign begging for money; it feels like he is saying, "Feel sorry for me and please give me your money."

One of the things that I like most about Habitat for Humanity is their sweat equity requirement, appropriately called a Hand Up and not a Hand Out. No one is given a free ride. Every family that gets a home must qualify by working a set number of hours toward the construction of not only their home but other recipients' homes as well. They must also meet the credit criteria to pay back the principal cost to build their home. This creates a sense of pride and ownership in those that participate.

If you are a parent, you may have noticed a lack of appreciation for the true value of money from your children (or perhaps, in all honesty, you may be able to recognize that in yourself). It is past time that we teach our children to earn their own way. Allow me to share an experiment that I read about that has stuck with me for many years.

First, give your child a certain amount of money. Take them shopping and don't influence their selection process. Pay close attention to what they buy and how fast their money will disappear. Next, create chores that will allow your child to earn the same amount of money that you had previously given them. Take them on another shopping trip. This time they will be spending money that they have earned. Place no restrictions on what they are allowed to buy. Watch their thought process this time. Often, they will not spend it all but if they do; they will be far more selective than previously. For yourself, allow yourself to spend only the amount of cash you have (say, for example, you withdraw $100 a month). You think a lot more about what you're buying when you hand over cash instead of a credit card.

The goal here is to teach America's future citizens to pay their own way. Don't ask others to feel sorry for you when you are totally capable of providing for yourself.

CHAPTER 11

FOCUSED

———————◆———————

HAVE YOU EVER been around an individual that appeared to be lost? They are present, but they seem to be in "la la" land. Sometimes this condition is caused by alcohol, drugs, a mental condition, or some trauma that has just happened. I can recall not remembering my actions after being told that my older brother had passed away. It was a shock to all of us.

In the business world, one of the biggest time wasters is meetings. However, if a meeting is planned and the agenda is followed while the attendees are focused on the subject matter, it can be of great value. It takes only one member of that meeting that is not zeroed in on the objective at hand to sabotage the entire meeting.

Would you want a member of a surgical team that was in the process of performing a major operation on you to be thinking about anything except the action they were about to undertake? It could be the difference of life or death. The same principal applies to major business decisions. A major wrong decision due to the lack of focus can bankrupt a company.

Let's take a moment and reflect on the minutes leading up to the Super Bowl kick-off. The teams are focused on the strategy that has been laid out for them by their coaches. Each team member has a roll to play.

If any member of that team doesn't deliver it could cost them the game. Most of the time, there is a last-minute huddle in the locker room where the entire team comes together and chants a slogan that creates a sense of unity with a mind's eye on winning. This helps to focus everyone on the job at hand.

Wars would never be won without a clear strategy or battle plan to achieve the objective. I believe that successful men and women know what they want and while they may not have a complete roadmap to get there, they usually know where to start and use many resources to blaze the trail toward their final objective while never losing site of the ultimate goal.

Remember, when you are in a meeting, you are, in one way or another, being judged by every other person in attendance. Never try to hide. Pick a seat that says you want to be there. Sit where you can make eye contact with as many people as possible, especially the person chairing the meeting. You'll more likely get their attention. And when you speak, you can see the reaction of others. Body language sometimes supersedes what we have to say. Look focused with the proper eye contact and proper physical gestures. Don't talk with your hands waving in every direction. Stick to the subject and stay focused.

Sometimes we need to remind our children to slow down, focus, and communicate in a way that we can understand the message they are trying to make. Perhaps we should practice what we preach! Are you focused?

CHAPTER 12

AIR HEADS (AKA OPPOSITE OF FOCUSED)

HAVE YOU EVER been called an "air head"? Maybe you have wanted to call someone an air head. If so, why do you think it happened? Often it is just a slang to gain the attention of the individual being named. From time to time, we all say or do senseless things. Often such actions take place when we are preoccupied by other thoughts. Or maybe we hear only a part of a discussion and feel compelled to add our two cents worth, which makes absolutely no sense. The phrase, "silence is golden" surely doesn't apply to us, right?

The point that we need to take to heart here is simple. DO WE TALK WHEN WE SHOULD BE LISTENING? Such actions will provide the basis for us to be labeled an air head.

Some people feel compelled to comment on any and every subject known to man. Often, they make statements that are false or only partially true. They leave you shaking your head and asking, "What is he talking about?" It only takes one such incident to make you distrustful of any future conversations with the individual.

We should remember that no one can argue with silence.

CHAPTER 13

ETHICAL

E THICS IS IN the mind of the beholder. We all have our own definition of the word. Often, we confuse it with what we we're taught or what we have read. I think it is far more personal. Perhaps it has more to do with our soul than all of the above. How do you define ethics? We are taught right from wrong based on the opinions of those that teach us. Are they, always right?

I had a twin brother. We were raised by the same parents at the same time. They taught us to be honest and always treat others as we would like to be treated. However, my twin brother and I had different ideas about most things. Often, I have contemplated why we thought so differently. His ethics were not the same as mine.

Very selflessly, I always thought that my opinion was generally correct. However, as I have aged, that attitude has mellowed. Quite often, I find myself thinking differently even from only a few years ago. Most human interactions are based on trust, honor, and respect for each individual. However, those values have been replaced with a desire to be successful or on top at whatever the cost. Many business and even personal decisions are made with little or no regard for what is right, only for personal gain.

Our generation was taught that "our name" was the most important thing in our life. We should protect our reputation and that of our family with great diligence. Never act or even give the appearance that you were involved in any unethical activity. Life is so much easier when you follow that rule. You never have to find ways to hide or cover up some activity.

The perfect epitaph on any headstone would read, "HERE LIES A PERSON THAT WAS HONEST AND ETHICAL THROUGHOUT THEIR LIFE."

CHAPTER 14

NATURAL SALESPERSON

━━━━━━━◆━━━━━━━

D O YOU KNOW any natural sales folks? What do you see that makes them fit into that category? Below is a list of some of the common traits of effective salespersons. Perhaps you can think of others.

- Confident
- Positive attitude
- Good communicator
- Smiles
- Listens
- Good speaker
- Product knowledge
- Knows when to close
- Refers to you by name
- Offers alternatives
- Not too pushy
- Explains benefits
- Doesn't become defensive
- Overcomes objections
- Truly appreciates the sale

- ⁺ Follows-up to ensure quality service
- ⁺ Understands their competition
- ⁺ Always striving to improve
- ⁺ Genuinely cares about the buyer
- ⁺ Is not greedy
- ⁺ Builds relationships
- ⁺ Quick to admit when they are wrong
- ⁺ Never too proud to apologize
- ⁺ Learns from their mistakes
- ⁺ Eager to do research for their clients
- ⁺ Projects honesty

It has been my experience that it is much harder to sell services versus products. Many services are hard to define and even harder to evaluate. Subjectivity enters the picture when the item being sold is not tangible. Many times, a service pays dividends well into the future and the immediate value is obscure. Therefore, it becomes harder to get a buy-in now. An example would be employee training. While it may cost time and some production during the process, the gain is long lived.

While we may not realize it, we are all salespeople. Everyday activities require us to buy and sell ideas. We are constantly trying to convince family members, friends, and business associates to accept our view. This is a major part of developing relationships. It is the essential ingredient of communications.

Those that have low self-esteem and project a negative attitude about life seem to have poor sales skills. Let's refer back to the previous mentioned list of traits found in good sales people. Grade yourself on a scale of 1-10 with 1 being the weakest and 10 the strongest.

How did you stack-up? How good of a salesperson are you?

CHAPTER 15

LIARS

I ONCE WORKED WITH a guy that would tell lie when the truth would have served his purpose much more effectively. After doing so, he had to continue the process to cover the first lie. Why do people feel that they cannot share good and bad news? Ultimately, not being honest completely destroys the integrity of the originator.

From time to time, we encounter people that we catch telling us lies or half-truths. When this happens, we can never completely trust them in the future. I will not do business with nor befriend a known liar.

If we unintentionally tell something that is not factual, it is our responsibility after we learn the correct facts to return to the individual(s) given the incorrect information as soon as possible and admit our mistakes. This will prevent the misinformation from being passed on to others and build even greater trust and respect for ourselves.

As I age and my hearing degenerates, often I misunderstand comments made directly to me, especially those made in group discussions. While it is embarrassing to ask folks to repeat themselves, it is truly the only way to ensure clear communication and thus preventing any sort of miscommunication.

I remember a sermon that was delivered in a small country church when I was young. It was about telling half-truths. The message emphasized the importance of not withholding information and only sharing the points that we want to make. This often misrepresents the entire subject. It is important to know all the facts when making business or personal decisions.

Quite frankly, withholding information is akin to lying by omission. Are you, on one level or another, a liar?

CHAPTER 16

ENVIRONMENTALIST

SOME MAY SAY there is a negative connotation attached to being known as a "tree hugger", but it is actually not a bad thing. Just think about the condition of our planet if we did not have people that were good stewards of our natural surroundings. When you consider all the beautiful trees, plants and different types of wildlife that have disappeared, it gives you a new prospective of those who go out of their way to protect what we have left.

Green Peace, Audubon Society, garden clubs, farmers, forest management companies, clean air commissions, and governmental oversite commissions are but a few of the organizations which help to keep the environment in check. While there are many federal, state, and local laws that are designed to protect our environment, often they are not enforced. The best way for us to do our part is to be careful not to pollute ourselves and to teach our children to be good citizens.

One of the best television ads I have ever seen told the story. It was silent with no caption. It showed an old American Indian sitting on his horse looking out over a polluted river. As the camera zoomed in on his face, it showed tears running down his wrinkled cheeks. In his heart, he was saddened by the careless activities of the generations that followed him. It is our personal responsibility as inhabitants of this world to protect it.

We should support environmentalist in their efforts to educate the public regarding pollution and practice being good stewards ourselves. Together we can bring about a better understanding of global warming and encourage our politicians to pass legislation that will save our environment for the future. Here are some ways that we can help:

+ Utilize solar or wind power vs. fossil fuel
+ Leave no trace behind (pick up and clean up behind ourselves)
+ Conserve energy (turn off lights and appliances when not in use)
+ Recycle (and teach recycling to our children)
+ Promote new technology (use energy efficient green construction standards)
+ Set our thermostats for reasonable comfort
+ Weatherize our homes (most local utility companies have programs to help)
+ Don't waste water (use brown water for lawn and plant irrigation)
+ Walk or bike on short trips (we don't need to drive to the mail box)
+ Whenever possible use biodegradable products

We should all do our part. Are you an environmentalist? I am.

CHAPTER 17

EXCELLENT SPEAKER

―――――◆―――――

THERE ARE MANY very good speakers. Two that come to my mind are President John Kennedy and President Ronald Reagan. While their delivery methods were different, each possessed the skills that demanded the audience's attention.

Let's list some of the attributes of excellent speakers:

- Speaks clearly
- Has a passion for their subject
- Uses vocabulary that the audience can understand
- Can be heard, but not too loud
- Doesn't preach or talk down to the audience
- Plans and practices before the speech
- Makes the presentation timely (not too lengthy)
- Delivers at the proper speed (doesn't talk too fast)
- Uses the proper jesters or body language
- Makes eye contact with different members of the audience
- Opens the speech with an interest grabber

- Uses intentional speaking and sticks to the subject (doesn't ramble)
- Ends the speech on a high note

How many more can you list? My Pastor is a very good speaker. He prepares and uses a written format. You can't tell that he is reading his sermon because he is so well prepared. On occasion, I have asked him for a copy of his sermon. He always provides it but with comments about the notes written in the columns and scratched over words. He explained that often he makes minor changes right up to the delivery time.

We can all learn to be better speakers. Dale Carnegie, Toast Masters and many self-help books can provide us with numerous tips. I attended BellSouth's Speakers Bureau Training; some of the suggestions they pointed out included the following:

- Know your audience
- Practice, practice, and practice again
- Study your subject
- Dress for the part
- Be organized
- Make no more than three points
- Start and end on time
- Leave your audience wanting to implement your suggestions
- Exhibit positive body language
- Never answer a question from the audience unless you absolutely know the answer

There are many electronic devices that can be used to enhance your presentation (i.e. computers, PowerPoint presentations, props, graphs, and charts). However, if there is an equipment breakdown or you don't fully know how to use the equipment, it can work against you. Part of being prepared includes always checking out the public announcement system, the podium location, and all other equipment before the audience begins to gather.

It is important to have a back-up plan just in case one of the previous mentioned fails.

Approach your talk as if you were talking to a friend or family member. Remember, you are the subject matter expert and have confidence in what you are about to share. Speak within your vocabulary. Never use words that you don't understand or can't even pronounce! If given the choice, talk about subjects that you enjoy and know a lot about.

When doing so, the words will come easy and you will do a great job!

CHAPTER 18

TOUGH

H AVE YOU EVER heard a person being referred to as being "tough"? It is used when individuals are dug-in on any subject which they are passionate. Often such folks show very little flexibility and are determined to sell their point. This characteristic could also be referred to as "stubborn."

There is a time when we should be tough. An example is disciplining our children. Have you ever heard the term "tough love"? When our son was twelve years old, he and a friend wanted to make extra money while out of school for the summer vacation. I had a new, very expensive riding lawn mower. He wanted to use it to mow lawns in the neighborhood. We discussed the importance of proper maintenance including checking the oil before cutting each lawn. He and his friend created a very successful summer business and had accumulated close to $3,000.

One afternoon when I arrived home from work, the lawn mower was in the drive-way. I was informed that the engine had stopped working. Upon examination we determined that it was out of oil. My son was honest and admitted that they had not been checking the oil on a regular basis.

The next day we loaded the mower on our trailer and took it to the shop where it had been purchased. The mechanic informed us that the motor was locked up due to the improper level of oil. The motor would have to be replaced. The cost of a new motor installed would cost around $800. It would be several days before the work could be completed but our son had scheduled more lawns to cut right away.

The shop had new mowers on sale that were the same make and model of the one that was in need of repair. The sale price was just over $1,600. Therefore, I decided that it would be a great lesson if my son purchased a new mower to replace the one that he had damaged. He would pay for it from the money that he had made during that summer. He didn't think it was fair for me to make him pay the full cost. Neither did his mother or his grandfather who offered to pay part of the bill. I stood my ground (being tough) and made him pay the full amount.

After that experience, he always, even to this day, has been extra careful to follow the maintenance schedule on all motorized equipment. A number of years later, when he entered college, he was pleasantly surprised to learn that I had deposited his lawn mower replacement cost into a savings account to be used toward his college expenses. He was appreciative of the lesson. He now has children of his own…I just wonder how tough he will be?

CHAPTER 19

HYPOCRITE

WEBSTER DEFINES A hypocrite as a dissembler or one given to false pretenses. Earlier in this book we talked about WANABES and Artificial and Cosmetic people. Perhaps these tend to blend with the Hypocrite or Liar. It is not a positive trait.

When I think of a hypocrite, I think of a person that means to do what is right but loses the courage or fortitude to carry through. This is often prevalent in alcohol and drug abusers. It is also noted in folks that are not strong or fail to think before they act. An example would be someone that volunteers to handle a task while in a group setting. However, once away from the lime light, they forget what they had agreed to do.

Quite often we promise ourselves through New Year's Resolutions, Wedding Vows, Oaths, and Pledges to commit to certain self-imposed standards. We do so with the best intentions. However, as our life and environment changes, we fail to follow through. While we never intended to do so, we become a hypocrite.

Perhaps this would be a better world if we were a little slower to make commitments beyond our reach. A smaller commitment met is far more valuable than a huge commitment that was missed. Be mindful of your commitments and do some self-reflection beforehand to ensure that you're not over-promising and under-delivering. Let's remember: once we lose the trust of an individual, it is very difficult to ever regain it!

CHAPTER 20

GOOD NEGOTIATOR

THERE IS A difference in being cheap verses a good negotiator. I have always liked a bargain and very seldom buy any large ticket items that are not on sale. However, my wife will never let me forget about the time that we found the perfect beach cottage located across the street from the Gulf of Mexico and directly on a fresh water lake. We watched it being built and knew it was meant for us. For some reason, construction stalled, and no activity took place for several weeks.

I did some investigation and learned that the builder was paying for the construction cost out of his pocket and had a cash flow problem. After approaching him and several weeks of negotiation, he finally agreed to accept our low offer. I was so proud of my negotiating skills that just a few days before we were schedule to close, I went back to him and demanded that he include a refrigerator with the deal. My wife felt that this was asking too much from the seller.

She was correct. Not only did the very kind gentleman refuse to add the refrigerator, but he backed out of the contract and told me that he would never sell me anything. You need to know when to hold them and when to fold them. We lost our dream cottage due to my demands.

Negotiating is an art. The secret is to make both sides feel they have won. It is important to move beyond each party's position and learn what their fundamental interest is. Often this can be accomplished by asking open-ended questions and asking in the proper tone. Great information gathering questions like, "I am curious about that, please explain it to me," or "What else?" can be used numerous times during the negotiating process. The more that you learn, the better you can negotiate.

Remember, you are trying to create a balance among all parties. The more people that are involved with different opinions; the greater the challenge. This is why most politicians work to get a number of cosigners on new legislation which they want to introduce. A minority doesn't rule; a compromise must be reached and agreed upon by all.

A specific and complete offer will enhance the likelihood that your offer will be accepted. It also raises the odds of generating an equally specific and detailed response. This increases the understanding of everyone. Do not play games. Be very clear as to what you are offering. You certainly want the same in a counter offer. The more we work at being a good negotiator, the better we become.

CHAPTER 21

A TRUE FRIEND

---◆---

IT HAS BEEN said that a true friend will tell you the truth and not just what you want to hear. Most of us claim that our spouse, parents, or siblings fall into this category. How many true friends do you claim? Are you someone's true friend?

Let's list some of the traits of a true friend:

- Trustworthy
- Honest
- Has your back
- Understands confidentiality
- Shares constructive criticism
- Forgives your mistakes
- Always ready to help when needed
- Doesn't expect payback for every favor they provide
- Looks for ways to please you
- Communicates well with you
- Stands up for you when you are not around
- Believes in you
- Shares life experiences

- Quick to say, "I am sorry"
- Loves you

Recently a man told me that he had no friends. I began to think about how sad that must be and wondered why he was without friends. All of a sudden it dawned on me: You must be a true friend before you can gain such a relationship.

We all have the same opportunity to build friendships, but we need to be very consciously working at it. Dale Carnegie's book "How to Win Friends and Influence People" is full of valuable tips that we need to practice daily. The most important trait that we all need to learn is to refrain from saying negative things about each other. As I stated earlier in the book, my mother would frequently tell us, "If you can't say something nice about a person, just don't say anything at all!"

While working on my will recently, a thought came to mind: who would be pallbearers at my funeral? I began to think about my true friends. I am very blessed with many, both men and women. They may need to have a lottery to pick only eight. It is a great feeling to rise each morning without having negative feelings toward anyone. The greatest book written tells us to love one another as Jesus loves us.

CHAPTER 22

MOTIVATOR

WHAT MOTIVATES YOU? How do you motivate others? The answers are not always the same. Some people seem to be self-starters and find ways to keep their interest fresh. They often are very successful in most anything they undertake. It all starts with a positive attitude. Is your attitude worth catching?

Let's list some of the traits of good motivators:

- Lead by example
- Good communicator
- Provides positive and negative feedback
- Gives timely feedback
- Praises publicly
- Criticizes privately
- Is a good mentor
- Is organized
- Plans their work and works their plan
- Is flexible
- Shares the game plan
- Listens

- Creates an eager want
- Accepts the responsibility
- Shows genuine appreciation

International studies have shown that money is not the best motivator for employees.

The Marcus Buckingham study revealed the following in order of importance:

- Workers rated interesting work as the most important to them
- Being appreciated
- Being in on things
- Job security
- High wages
- Promotion and growth
- Working conditions
- Loyalty of supervisor
- Help with personal problems
- Tactful discipline

It has been my experience, that the greatest motivator is empowering individuals to make their own decisions. None of us like to be micro-managed. It is true that this opens the door for mistakes, however if we learn from them we will grow in our own leadership skills and ability to motivate others.

CHAPTER 23

CARING AND SHARING

◆

WHAT CAUSES SOME people to be more benevolent than others? It has always interested me when conducting United Way and other non-profit fundraisers: The individuals with the least seem to give the most. Maybe they understand the need. It goes back to the old adage: "Walk a mile in my shoes".

Most of us were taught at a very early age to share. It started with toys, games and most of all the attention of our parents and teachers. I have read that children with no siblings often have a harder time sharing. That is not always the case. My wife and I had one child. He was big and stands 6' 3" as a man. His nature has always been to help those that are smaller, and he never uses his size to his advantage except when playing football.

We tried to lead by example. At a very early age we taught our son to give to the church, charities, and people in need. We pointed out homeless folks and those that were down on their luck. At Christmas, we would find a family that needed help and put together food baskets and small gifts for the children. Our son would go with us to deliver the gifts.

As a young teenager, he was involved with Air Force Junior Reserve Officers Training Corps. His group did a number of community projects and activities to raise money. One such project involved raising funds to build a state of the art playground. Today the park has a very visible plaque recognizing their efforts. I can remember talking to our son and his buddies about why they were spending so much time and energy on the park. They were unanimous in the answer, "Because we care. We care that children with handicaps have a safe place to play."

When you think about it, there are three reasons that we give to a cause: 1) we believe in the mission that we are supporting; 2) a family member or friend ask us to participate; and 3) we react to a television ad, billboard or other media presentation that touches our soul.

The greatest book written teaches us to give. Most church goers recognize a 10% tithe should be given back to the church. I remember a story about a woman that gave two copper coins and it was noted that her gift was greater than the wealthy that gave much more. She gave all that she had with a cheerful heart. The heartfelt reason for giving is worth more than the gift. We should all remember that we can never give more than has been given to us. Recently, I read that if you share a windfall or extra items with others: it is not truly giving. A true gift is when you make a sacrifice to give and do it with the right attitude.

CHAPTER 24

PERFECTIONIST

S OME THINGS REQUIRE perfect work. Examples would be brain surgery, launching rockets, bowling a score of 300 or pitching a no-hitter. It should be our inner work standard to strive for perfection while also allowing room for mistakes, as long as we learn from them. Thank God, most of us have jobs that will allow us to make a few mistakes along the way.

My older brother after finishing a stint in the Army went to work for a die-tool company. His job was to assist in manufacturing dies that were used in presses to precisely cut metal into parts used to manufacture automobiles. It was important that these dies have no flaws. The reason being the slightest inaccuracy could result in stopping the assembly line.

Later he went into the business of restoring old furniture, pianos, and organs. The habits that he learned as a die tool specialist carried over to his new profession. It was essential that the restoration work be as near to the original as possible. This generated within him a sense of perfectionism.

Many years later after he had retired and bought a second home in Florida, he assisted me with repairs on our rental properties. On several occasions he and I had disagreements over the quality of work that we were doing which sometimes created unnecessary expenses. An example was the installation of new interior doors in a used mobile home. While I was comfortable with our first installation, he insisted that we reinstall the doors to meet his specifications. After working together for a period of time, he realized most of the projects we were working on did not require the same level of perfection of which he was accustomed.

All of us have certain areas in which we strive for perfection. Generally, these areas are treated with a higher priority. An example that comes to mind is Christmas dinners at our house. My wife wants everything to be perfect. Perhaps it would be appropriate to suggest that we all possess a certain level of perfectionism.

CHAPTER 25

TALENTED

C AN YOU DRAW, paint, sing, dance, or quote volumes of lines in a play? Most of us have some type of talent. Isn't it interesting that the more we use our talents, the better they become?

Let's see how many different talents that we can list:

- Excellent cook
- Public speaking
- Gardening
- Writer
- Singing
- Dancing
- Story telling
- Teacher
- Painting
- Designer
- Automotive mechanic
- Computer guru
- Wood craftsman
- Fisherman

- Hunter
- Airplane pilot
- Diver
- Planner
- Animal trainer
- Any sport in which you excel
- Musician
- Healthcare Professional
- Make up artist
- Hairdresser
- Seamstress
- Welder
- Surgeon
- Care taker
- Minister
- Banker

These are but a few of the many different talents that we develop. Many of our pets can be taught to do tricks of which we are very proud to show off: "Look, my dog can stand on her back legs and walk, or, my horse can take a bow." My point is simply many talents can be taught. My wife plays the piano and her brother plays a guitar, and they were both taught to do so.

We need to look for things that interest us and dedicate part of our 1,440 minutes each day toward developing our skills to be our very best in that area. Often middle age or older folks change their career to do something that they have always wanted to do, just by focusing on perfecting their talent in an area that they love. Life is very short, and I truly believe that it can be extended when a person is at peace with themselves and spend most of their time doing something that they enjoy.

Are you happy? How do you use your talents to better yourself and perhaps even others?

CHAPTER 26

PROCRASTINATORS

DO YOU WAIT to the very last minute to complete a task or continuously arrive late to a scheduled event or meeting? I like to operate on Lombardi time, which is fifteen minutes early. The famous coach insisted that his players were always at practice, team meetings and other functions a quarter hour before the advertised starting time.

This practice has been beneficial to me in many ways. It gives me a buffer of time to handle unforeseen events, i.e. accidents, highway traffic, specific event location changes and weather. It also provides me with better seating selection and an opportunity to familiarize myself with my surroundings which will help me to focus on the subject matter.

My theory is that one reason some folks procrastinate is simply a delay tactic to cover up their lack of preparedness. Perhaps they feel that a question unanswered will solve itself in due time. Another reason is lack of planning or time management. Whatever the reason, it is a distraction when late arrivers enter the room after the program has started. Some meetings are delayed to accommodate late arrivals. It shows no respect for those that were on time. When this happens, I want to get up and walk out.

Have you ever considered the rippling effect of procrastination?

Often in the business world, you cannot start your part of a project until you receive information from other members of the team. If they are late, you are placed in a stressful position to get the project completed on time. We must respect the overall impact that our procrastination could have on the entire business.

One out-of-sequence individual on an assembly line can shut down the factory. Let's not make people wait on us!

CHAPTER 27

ACCUMULATORS

S OME PEOPLE NEVER throw anything away. They accumulate junk. Many times, what is being collected has very little true value. When a person grows up in poverty, they place more value on almost everything. They grew up making do with whatever they had and were taught to recycle. We did it in our home.

My dad was always making something out of nothing. My twin brother and I had the job of pulling nails from used lumber and straightening them to be reused. I can't recall my dad ever having new nails. He also made dog collars or collars for his goats from worn leather belts. Parts of old shoes were used when making slingshots.

My mother saved every plastic milk jug and jars of all sizes and shapes. She used them over and over when making jams, jellies, and sweet pickles. I remember neighbors collecting jars to give her. She would remove all the buttons and zippers from worn out clothes and use them to mend or fashion new ones. We loved to play with her button collection. She taught us to count the buttons at a very young age. Additionally, many women of that period would save cloth scrapes to be recycled when making quilts. Flour sacks and feed sacks were printed in colors and prints, thus providing material that could be used to make clothing. I remember well, shirts made from flour and feed sacks.

Most of our neighbors that had vegetable gardens would keep seeds from their crops each year to be used the following year when planting. Mother did the same with many of her flowers. It was a common practice to share your seeds with family and friends.

Most current day collectors do so as a hobby and not out of necessity. Coins, stamps, guns, fishing equipment, art and many other items are collected. My wife collects White House Christmas Ornaments. They each are part of a limited edition and comes with a history lesson. One day her collection will be valuable, and our grandchildren will appreciate her efforts.

A few years ago, I was fortunate to be part of a group that made a visit to Alaska. We boarded the Alaska Railroad in Anchorage. As we made our way through the wilderness to Fairbanks, it was rare to see a cabin or home because of the remoteness of the railroad. We had a young female college student as our guide. She used the stage name of "SunShine". As she pointed out different items of interest, someone asked her why all the houses that we could see were surrounded with old junk cars, trucks, tractors, and other garbage. Her answer was that it was a sign of wealth. People saved everything to recycle. You can't run over to the hardware store and pick up a bolt or screw, so they keep everything.

Some of the more valuable collectables include family pictures or home movies. These provide a source of understanding for the following generations. They say that a picture is worth a thousand words. Other family heirlooms such as furniture, homemade quilts, cooking recipes, old books, tools, and any item that has a special meaning is worth preserving.

One of the intangible priceless collectibles that come to my mind is "stories", the history of our family members that we cherish. I can remember stories being told about my great grandparents. We need to pass these along for the benefit of generations to come.

What do you collect and why?

CHAPTER 28

HEALTH CONSCIOUS

I T IS IMPORTANT that we all practice good health habitats. We are taught at a very young age basic hygiene, to brush our teeth, take regular baths, wash our hands before we eat, don't eat things that are picked up off the floor, cover our mouths when we sneeze, and many other good-sense practices.

As we age, we begin to focus on our personal health. Regular dental appointments often lead to visits to specialist such as oral surgeons, orthodontists, or cosmetic dentistry. The need to maintain healthy teeth is drilled into us as children.

Skin care becomes more of an issue with age. Exposure to the sun over the years brings about a real need for frequent examinations, particularly for those who work outside. Skin cancer has become a serious possibility; caught early, it can be treated, and lives saved.

We have so many options regarding new and improved products that can be purchased over the counter, not to mention all that our doctors may prescribe. There are many vitamins, supplements and holistic medical treatments which are easily accessible.

Around the age of 40, something happens to our eyes. Many of us need to use glasses to read. In today's environment, we need help to best use our computers. The new technology provides a number of options including corrective surgery, contact lenses and special glasses and other treatments.

What did you say? I didn't understand. These are but a few of the repeated statements that indicate a lack of hearing. I happen to believe that the loud noise that we are all subjected to in our every day lives impacts our hearing. Traffic, airplanes, loud radios and almost every device makes noise. We block out sounds that we don't need, which often causes us to not hear important data.

All of these things make up our health universe. They are interdependent. The loss of one sense has a direct influence on others. I have read that a blind person generally has a greater hearing ability or a superior sense of feeling and sense of smell. Perhaps we have a tendency to use whatever we have to replace those that are missing.

Exercise and a proper diet contribute to good health. Most Americans could afford to lose a few pounds. It has been said that no one can take care of your body better than you. Do you make your health a priority?

CHAPTER 29

RESOURCEFUL

WHEN I THINK of a resourceful person, I think of someone that is very flexible and willing to take a chance on substituting items or thoughts that are different from the norm. Many times, throughout history, great achievements have been accomplished through being resourceful.

Adapting to change is not easy but often lays the groundwork for a much better result. I can remember my mother using a different ingredient in a recipe simply because she did not have the recommended item. Milk instead of cream, margarine instead of butter are a few examples. President Theodore Roosevelt stated it best when he said, "Do what you can with what you have where you are".

My wife's grandmother was very resourceful. She made all the birthday and Christmas gifts for family members. She was raised on a very rural South Alabama farm where she learned at a young age to improvise. It has been said that the value of a gift is in the heart of the giver.

As a child, often we would play games with sticks, rocks, cardboard boxes, cans, and string. We even made kites from newspaper and wet flour for glue. Believe it or not they flew just as well as the neighbors' store-bought model.

Our older sisters would cut paper dolls from the Sears catalog and play for hours. They made imaginary cookies on a make-believe stove. We would share them and brag about how good they tasted. I just thought about something: their cookies had no calories!

My mother's father enjoyed whittling (better know as carving) with his little pocket knife. He took special care of that little knife. He spent hours sharpening both blades on a stone and then using a leather strap to put the final edge on each. He would tell us children that a dull knife would cut you, but you would respect a sharp one and never be cut. Granddaddy would sit in an old porch swing and whittle all types of little animals for us. He made grandmother a special wooden spoon that she used when making some of our favorite meals.

Our mother could take leftovers from a previous meal, add a few things, and make it wonderful. She had a gift when it came to being resourceful. While our economic situation dictated the need to do so; it seemed to be something that she enjoyed. Everyone wanted to be invited to our house for a meal.

Today, we live in a throwaway society. If we were truly resourceful, we could feed a hungry world. On a scale of 1 to 10, what is your resourcefulness grade?

CHAPTER 30

GREAT HOST / HOSTESS

W E HAVE ALL visited someone that has made us feel so comfortable that we really don't want to leave. They posses an almost forgotten talent. Many are taught the skills, but few are able to implement them without coming across as artificial or cosmetic. Great hosts or hostesses are those individuals that have a natural way of making you feel at home or totally at ease when you are a visitor.

While growing up, I was always ready to visit our Aunt Bertha. She was my mother's youngest sister and had a bond with mother. Aunt Bertha and her husband, Riley, had one son. He was a couple years older than my twin brother and I. Every time that we would go to their house, Aunt Bertha would hug and kiss us and tell us how much we had grown. She always had positive things to say.

Additionally, she would spend some time with us. Maybe we would make cookies or Kool-Aid or read a bible story. She smiled all the time and made you smile. She taught her son to mentor us and spend time sharing his toys. Time would fly by when we were at their house. We were never ready to go home when the time arrived.

On the other hand, mother had another sister which you never felt comfortable around.

She was a perfectionist and always had to find something wrong with everything. "Your hair looks good, BUT..." or, "I like your shirt, BUT it is too big for you." There were very few times that I was around her that I didn't get my feelings hurt. We tried to find reasons not to visit.

Our mother and grandmother were absolutely the perfect hostesses. It didn't matter if you were invited or just dropped in. Almost every Sunday, someone from church would come to our house to visit. Often this would include lunch. Mother would welcome them into the kitchen and often put them to work helping to prepare for the extra people.

We had a garden and sometimes we would be sent out to pick more tomatoes, corn or an additional basket of peas. Dad might clean another chicken to be cooked. It would delay the meal being served but it was worth the wait. Everyone enjoyed mother's hospitality.

In today's busy environment, most of us just don't have the time to be a good host or hostess. It is much easier to eat out or order in. The most important ingredient when entertaining guests is simply to make enough time to enjoy each other.

My recommendations to be a great host or hostess? Stage the meal to allow time to meet and greet and share quality time together. This should be followed with a menu that takes all attendees into consideration.

The next step is proper seating. It is best to rotate a man next to a woman around the table. To allow for opportunities to learn more about each other, separate husbands and wives. Make the setting simple and comfortable.

Be sure that everyone is properly introduced before the meal. It is better if you can be sure that known enemies are not mixed. Put them at opposite ends of the table. Better, don't invite both of them to the same event. Always thank your guest for visiting and invite them back again. Don't mix business with pleasure.

There are many good books on this subject. However, the best rule is to treat your guest the way you want to be treated as a guest. You should pay attention to the body language and the compliments or lack thereof from your guest. A smile, handshake or parting hug speaks louder than words.

With a little effort, we can all become good hosts and hostesses. Plan an event and get started!

CHAPTER 31

SUCCESSFUL MONEY MANAGER

I T ISN'T ALWAYS how much money that you have but rather how you spend it. There is an art to managing your resources; balancing spending on needs vs. pleasure. Too much in either direction can destroy the other. Additionally, the habit of saving on a regular basis is a must.

My older sister had the ability to stretch a dollar. Long before computers, she examined the Wednesday newspaper to learn the weekly specials at all the major grocery stores. First, she would make up a meal menu for the following week. Next, she checked the pantry to determine what items were needed to provide the following weeks meals. After making her shopping list, she searched the paper to find the best buys.

Perhaps the next step was the most important. She planned her shopping to allow her to take the most direct route to the stores. Once she arrived at store number one, she took the list of sale items and/or coupons for that store only. She focused only on the items on the list. This process was repeated at the next grocery store and finally finished at the third location. Rarely did she buy anything that was not on the list.

This type of discipline resulted in more groceries for less money. Simple things like day old bread, bent cans, and ripe fruit (sold at discounted prices) aided her savings. She also shopped consignment stores for her family's clothing. She did all of her housework and taught her sons to keep up the lawn. Lights were turned off when you left a room and the heating and cooling was set to save energy. These traits were passed on to her sons.

My wife and I have dabbled in real estate for a number of years. We have learned that your money is made at the time that you purchase property, not just when you sell it. If you pay too much to begin with, odds are that you will not recover your cost and definitely not make any money. Another important factor is your debt service. What is it costing you to borrow money? The old saying, "The rich get richer" is so true. The number one reason is that those with money can pay cash and have no debt service to pay.

Impulsive buying can break the bank. People buy things that they don't need and will not use. Successful money mangers seem to have greater control over impulsive buying. Instead of jumping on the first opportunity to purchase something just because it is on sale, they determine the true value or use for the family or business.

I have never seen a successful money manager that did not have a budget. Many of them have both short and long-term budgets. Budgets must be continually updated. The cost of products and services are forever changing. Unexpected expenses (medical costs, accidents, natural disasters and many other unknowns) cause our budgets to change. Sometimes we enjoy a windfall which adds to our income. This may allow for budget changes.

All of us should pay our taxes; however, some people are late doing so, which incurs a penalty. This is an unnecessary expense. Good money managers know when their taxes are due and if any discounts are available for paying early (property taxes in Florida). They take advantage of these savings.

Many times, you can receive a discount if you pay your insurances a year at a time instead of monthly. The same is true for newspaper and magazines subscriptions. AARP, Senior and Military Discounts and other memberships provide additional savings if used. Smart people take advantage of every opportunity to save a nickel. Make a list of other ways that you can be thrifty.

It is important to periodically review your banking actives. Are you getting the most interest on your money? Sometimes a money market account will pay more than a savings account. Some banks have free checking if you maintain the proper balance in your account. On the flip side, how much interest are you paying for money that you have borrowed? Paying 12+% on debt while earning less than 2% on savings isn't very smart. Shopping can pay more on your savings and save more on your loans. This should be reviewed annually.

When I was young, we were taught to work and save toward the purchase of items that we desired. We just didn't buy things on credit. This made whatever we purchased seem more valuable. The wait associated with earning and saving enough to pay cash would on occasion make you realize that the particular item was not really needed. Perhaps that same process should be followed as adults.

There is another important point that is made in a famous book. It refers to giving back 10% of your earnings to worthy causes. The book teaches that we will be repaid tenfold. My wife and I have always practiced this rule and we believe it truly works.

It has been said, "We are born to learn, learn to earn and earn to return!" Where are you in this process?

CHAPTER 32

FLIRTATIOUS

I GREW UP IN an environment where it was normal for individuals to greet each other with a hug. This was a common practice for both men and women. It was always done as a sincere gesture without ulterior motives. Handshakes were generally part of the greeting as well as the parting. However, today this activity could be used against you. People have changed, and they no longer accept or practice yesterday's habits. Everyone is so sensitive to lawsuits or individual rights that we have almost erased an American tradition.

Isn't it interesting how children want to hug their loved ones or their pet? We teach them to hug grandma and grandpa, and other children after a fight. It just seems to be a natural way of communicating. On the other hand, teaching our children to wink or make flirtatious advances can develop into an unforeseen problem. I have never believed in kissing and making up after children have a misunderstanding. They should apologize and promise not to repeat the same mistake.

Have you ever been around a person that flirts their way to achieve their objective? It is very degrading to all parties. We should all smile and be gracious. However, a wink or any other suggestive gesture is not appropriate. We should communicate directly in a professional manner showing respect for every individual.

The way that we dress could be interpreted as flirtatious. This is particularly true in the workplace. Showing too much cleavage or wearing clothing that is revealing certainly distracts and could lead to suggestive thoughts. This technique has been used throughout the ages for the purpose of gaining individual attention or to advance an agenda.

It would be unnatural to think that we are never attracted to other people. We are! That within itself is not the problem. How we handle the attraction becomes the question.

As leaders, we need to set the example as to our dress and actions. I once worked with a lady that would follow every request with a wink. I had to ask her to stop doing so when communicating with me as I felt it was unprofessional. She was offended by my request and felt that she had the right to do whatever she liked. After explaining to her that she had a choice: stop winking or find another job, she stopped.

CHAPTER 33

POLITICIAN

◆

W E ARE ALL politicians. Some have the titles. Your popularity changes with the title. I should know. A number of years ago, a couple of my political friends talked me into running for the County Commission. We did and won. I was a good ol' boy the day before the election and one of those cheating scoundrels the day after I was elected. You give up almost all your and your family's private life once elected.

The truth of the matter is that no one person can make much of a difference alone. You must create alliances for common causes that will provide a majority vote. Nothing can be accomplished on your own. When we study the history of our nation, we learn of many great debates by very passionate politicians regarding laws that they wanted to change or implement. It never happened without a majority vote. Most of the time, compromise is the only answer. I once read that the only good law that is passed is one that disappoints both sides.

There is a difference between a statesman and a politician. A statesman has a talent that provides the skills to communicate and compromise. None of us can, nor should, always get exactly what we want. Often, we are not really sure of ourselves. A statesman will ask others their opinion and find a way to blend them with his own. Most times this makes for a better outcome. A good example is the writing of the Constitution of the United States of America.

Most politicians push hard for what they want and accept nothing less. This causes many governing bodies to produce little to no quality legislation. It creates a biased and unfriendly environment. A couple of years ago, such action caused the US Government to shut down operations because a compromise could not be reached on the budget. This cost all tax payers a tremendous amount of money and put our national security at risk.

As in politics and government at all levels, no business or family can exist without some compromise. Take a minute to think of some comprises that you have made recently.

CHAPTER 34

SUPERSTITIOUS

M ANY PROFESSIONAL SPORTS participants wear the same socks, jersey, lucky necklace, or some other item because they feel it will bring them good luck. Many golfers will only use a special putter. Some baseball players have a routine that they perform before stepping into the batter's box. All of these actions are a figment of the imagination regarding making a difference in the outcome.

I don't walk under ladders. It is not because I am superstitious. It is because it is not safe. I don't want the ladder to fall on me. Others feel that it will bring about bad luck. The same is true if you spot a penny on the ground with the "tails" showing. Many will not pick it up. Some folks are afraid to travel over a place where they have just witnessed a black cat cross.

Have you ever heard that seven is a lucky number? It was my little league baseball number. I thought it was lucky because the great Babe Ruth wore the same number. However, it did not propel me to the all-stars. Some believe the number thirteen is an unlucky number. Some hotels skip thirteen when numbering each floor. Many great football quarterbacks have worn the number thirteen and it didn't influence their game.

Most of us associate a good or successful outcome with something that has helped us. Does this make us superstitious? If you believe that the particular activity works for you, then use it. Many times, our actions are more of a habit than superstition. Have you ever heard that if you get up on the wrong side of the bed that you will have a bad day? Well, just which side is the wrong side? It must be in the mind of each individual.

My father-in law was a great fisherman. He had special lures that he knew would help him catch fish. He would refer to the Farmer's Almanac to learn the best time of the day to fish. Additionally, he believed that the stage of the moon had a direct bearing on the number of fish he would catch. Was he superstitious? It has been said if you believe something enough that it will come to pass. I call it faith.

CHAPTER 35

RADICALS

WEBSTER DEFINES RADICAL as: 1) fundamental, complete, thorough; extreme; 2) revolutionary, abrupt. We often hear people say that someone is just a radical.

Does that mean that they have very definite ideas about a given subject and are willing to debate just about anyone to defend their position? Most of the time when I refer to someone as a radical, it portrays an individual that becomes so passionate about their beliefs that they refuse to listen to any other view. They will use a number of tactics to push their agenda, of which many might border-line on being hostile.

Many radicals are overcome by religious and/or political doctrine. They almost do not have a mind of their own but instead are caught up in the movement. It is like a pep rally at a high school or college football game…it is easy to get caught up in the euphoria of the moment. Everyone wants to be a part of the crowd and there is no thought process used. We just go along with the activities of the moment. The environment changes us, and we become something other than ourselves. Often, we can reflect back and say, "Did I really do that?" As humans, we are all capable of acting in ways that normally we would not do, and later wonder why we made such a thoughtless decision.

We need to have deep convictions for which we will stand. Otherwise, we have no real purpose in life. This does not give us a license to demand others to think like us. It would be a very dull world if we all thought alike.

Growing up we were taught to respect God, America, and our elders. There was no compromise. Perhaps the hard times that most people faced during World War I, the great depression and World War II had a sobering effect. Everyone needed something to believe in and rally around. We did not have television and radio commentaries thinking for us. Folks tended to listen to those older who had experienced many hardships. There was genuine respect for others.

Today, everything must be politically correct. Any and everything goes, regardless of who might be negatively affected. It seems to be fashionable to disrupt, protest, or destroy common sense values at the expense of everyone. It is my life and I can do whatever I want, just get out of my way!

Many of my friends have become very polarized along political party lines. America was founded and has prospered by doing what is best for the nation, not what is best for political parties. We should all be Americans first and party members next. The strained relationship between political parties in our federal government has cost tax payers billions of dollars. It is past time that our congressional leaders stop being radicals and reach across the aisle with compromising efforts for the betterment of all Americans. Are you a Radical?

CHAPTER 36

PET LOVERS

H OW CAN ANYONE mistreat any animal? My parents taught us that is was a sin to do so. I can't be the judge of that; however, I do feel that every breathing creature has its place and should be respected as such. I have always felt that you can determine the soul of a person by the way they treat their pets.

Some of us perhaps do too much for our pets. The Telephone Pioneers (an organization made up of active and retired telephone company employees), started collecting food for pets several years ago. It was not to be given directly to the Humane Society but instead delivered to those receiving meals on wheels. You might ask why. The answer was simple. Those receiving meals for their use were giving most of it to their pets and doing without themselves. It was learned that many times pet owners, partially those that live alone with a pet, will eat more and enjoy a meal if they eat with their pets.

Some folks have a desire to own exotic animals. There are federal, state and local laws that restrict such ownership. These are designed to protect people from being harmed by wild or dangerous animals. Also, they are meant to protect the animals. Many species can't survive in captivity. Nature has a pecking order. The strongest survive without man interfering. Pay attention to pet owners. Often, they have a physical resemblance, hair style or dress to mimic their pets. Fat people have fat pets, etc.

Many pets are trained to be care givers and play an important role in the quality of life for their masters. We should all be aware of service dogs and other trained animals that make such a difference in peoples' lives. The military has mastered such use with birds, dolphin, dogs, and beast of burden (mules, etc.)

Often, when playing and talking with our family Poodle, I wonder just how much she understands. Half of all pet owners in the United States admit to talking to their pets as if they were children. Her undivided attention and devoted love is worth more than I can explain. She is always there to greet us with the same happy smile, tail wagging and a special bark that says, "Welcome home, I sure missed you"! How could you ever mistreat a pet that is that sweet?

The internet tells us that the United States has more dogs and cats as pets than any other country. However, Brazil is number one when it comes to birds, followed by Italy and then the United States. The fourth largest pet ownership is fish with the United States leading all other countries.

Americans spend over $50 billion per year on their pets and over 27% of American pet owners admit to having had a professional photo taken with their pets.

Often parents purchase pets for their children for the purpose of introducing them to the work associated with care giving. This is an important part of child development. Later in life as we grow old, the same pet connection can bring healing or pleasure to us. The attitude that people show toward animals often reflect their attitude toward other people.

CHAPTER 37

CAREGIVERS

SOME PEOPLE CHOSE to be professional caregivers while others are forced to do so after an accident or health deterioration of a family member. The professional generally is trained to cope with the many challenges and can leave the stress after a day's work. On the other hand, family members and loved ones that are forced into the position are very seldom trained or prepared for what is in store. They lack the ability to walk away and rest their body and mind.

A few years ago, First Lady Rosalynn Carter came to our community and gave a speech to honor caregivers. She talked about burn out and the need for caregivers to receive help. No one understands the 24 hours per day stress that is placed upon those that live in a household where they are the primary caregiver. Her message was to the point: Caregivers need our help!

Perhaps, one of the most precious gifts that any of us could give would be to find ways to assist caregivers. Relieve them for a few hours at the time. A number of organizations provide a day or better yet, a weekend, to allow the caregiver a chance to rest and recharge.

You might ask; how does caregiver fit in this book of personalities? The answer is simple. Not everyone can be a caregiver. It takes a lot of love, passion, and knowledge to do the right thing for those that need us. This can be a learned by some. It requires a special caring person to develop such skills. However, you must start with a willing personality. Do you have what it takes?

CHAPTER 38

PESSIMISTIC

❖

IS YOUR GLASS half full or half empty? Some folks have a negative outlook on life. The sky is falling, doom day is about here. They have a hard time finding good in anything. I had an Aunt that was that way. I often wondered how her children could tolerate always being corrected and hardly ever receiving positive reinforcement from their mother.

While going through "Boot Champ" in the Army, you expected to be harassed by your drill sergeant. It was impossible to do anything right as part of your training. They were determined to break you and make you feel helpless. After a while, you stopped thinking and became part of a machine that was operated by your superiors.

It is easy to point out short comings of others. We do it with out thinking. Look at her hair, he is so fat, I would never wear those clothes. The comments are endless. Some people seem to enjoy correcting others or simply gossiping for no reason except to be heard.

Our father, unlike mother, seemed to focus on the hard times. He was pleased with the status-queue and didn't exhibit much of a desire to improve. He would complain when Mother would make improvements to our home, that everything cost too much, and we were perfectly fine without the change. Often, his attitude would take away from the enjoyment of other family members.

From time to time, I am involved in fund raising projects for our church or other not for profit groups in our community. Generally, we have a committee or group that work together. It is very dishearten to have a member of the team that feels that we just cannot meet our goal. I would prefer that they go some place else and let the rest of us get the job done.

We need to work toward guarding against being a pessimistic. Others, partially children will pick up our attitudes. Let's work to find the good in people and activities around us.

Find ways to compliment achievements of others. The more we do the easier it becomes, and we will be more fun to be around.

CHAPTER 39

SKEPTIC

HAVE YOU EVER been around a person that questions every statement or action taken by those near them? It reminds me of our son at about the age of four. Why Dad...but why; seemed to be his response to all of my instructions. It is understandable that children must ask question to be able to learn. However, it just isn't natural as an adult to quiz or challenge everything that we are told or read.

During my career at the Telephone Company, often I did not fully understand the technical aspects regarding the transmission of voice and data. However, I learned to follow instructions and to read circuit drawings. It was important to trust the engineers and not to try to become a subject matter expert with each of the over 2000 products and services that we offered.

On the flip side, we should use common sense when being offered something that is too good to be true. Don't buy ocean front property is Arizona, or expect to win the lottery every time we purchase a ticket.

Some skepticism is important. We should do research to gain enough knowledge to make sound decisions. Generally, we want to get a second opinion before having any major surgery or making important investments.

Sometimes we study things to death. Too much information causes confusion. I had a boss that would say, "Tell me what time is it; don't build a clock!" have you ever been around someone that always took way too much time to answer a simple question? We have a tenancy to not ask them very many questions.

Trust eliminates skepticism. When you are challenged on most of your thoughts, it gives you the feeling that the challenger just doesn't trust what you are saying. It is important to remember that if we ever lose a person's trust, it is very difficult to ever regain it.

Pay attention for your reasons for showing skepticism. Is it because of information or gossip that we have learned through the media or a third party? Perhaps, we should do our own homework and learn to trust each other. Let's work at it!

CHAPTER 40

INTROVERTED

H AVE YOU EVER heard the statement that he or she was afraid of their own shadow? This probably exaggerates their true behavior. However, many children tend to be very shy and often hide when introduced to strangers. Most of them will grow to be surer of themselves and more socially active.

Webster describes an introvert to be one completely absorbed in his own thoughts and dreams to the exclusion of the outer world or to turn inward; be unduly concerned with one's own thoughts.

This definition has made me rethink just what is happening with folks that seem to want to be alone and refuse to take the lead in any event. I have often considered it to be a weakness. However, some of the worlds' greatest inventors, writers, physicians, scientist, and thinkers worked alone. It is part of their personality. Therefore, what I have perceived to be a weakness may be a strength for some people.

Our oldest sister liked to read. She spent a lot of time alone, practically after losing her husband to cancer. She did an excellent job raising two sons on her own. Maybe she just didn't have the time for much of a social life. However, I would have liked to have seen her be more involved in things that I thought would make her happy. At times, I mislabeled her to be an introvert.

Being an introvert will limit some career opportunities. An example would be a salesperson. You must be outgoing and initiate conversation related to the product that you are trying to sell. Can you imagine going to a car lot to buy a car and spotting the salesperson standing next to any object and trying to hide, so they would not have to talk to you? They would not hold that job very long. Can you think of other careers where an introvert would not fit?

On the flip side, there are many jobs in research and development which require very little interaction with others. I feel that the use of computers drives people into their own little world, thus creating more introverts. While at Disney World this past week, I observed many young children being pushed around in their strollers playing games on their parents' cell phones or small computers. They were totally ignoring the festivities going on around them. How can we expect the next generations to know how to be anything but introverts?

At some point in our lives, we have all done or said something that embarrassed us. We would like to take it back or redo our action. Such activities make us want to hide. However, the best way to recover is to admit our wrong doings and make a sincere effort to not make the same mistake again.

A number of years ago, some of my business friends talked me into running for County Commissioner. After consulting with my family and employer, I agreed.

We assembled a campaign team and went to work. Several months later, we had won the Primary and General election by a rather large margin. This was a tremendous boost to my ego. Later, one of my closest friends told me that I got, "The Big Head".

After serving a four-year term, I decided to run for reelection. I was sure that I would win. However, I lost with 48% of the vote. I was embarrassed, not only for myself but my family and those that had worked very hard on the campaign. I wanted to move out of the County to some place where no one knew me. The circumstances turned me into an introvert. All I could think about was me and what made me fail.

Thanks to a loving wife that got me busy on other community projects, I was able to become my old self again. Have you had experiences that have made you to become an introvert? How did you recover?

CHAPTER 41

PHILANTHROPIST

D O YOU HAVE to be rich to be a philanthropist? Based on the media, it certainly seems so. We rarely see a television reporter or a newspaper article that shares stories of small but meaningful acts of kindness. Many take place daily without any recognition. Perhaps these are often done in obscurity. Many people do not want publicity regarding gifts or contributions of any size. They feel that it will bring a flood of requests from many other individuals of agencies.

The media has made such to do about very wealthy companies or individuals making billions of dollars in gifts that have a particular cause. Some examples include Bill Gates Foundation. He and his wife have chosen third world countries which are overrun by poverty to focus their giving. Recently I saw a television program that featured several billionaires which had created a club and challenged others throughout the world to join them in giving a large portion of their wealth back to common causes, such as a cure for a number of health issues.

I have known several philanthropists. The three that come to mind all are deceased; however, each of them established foundations to manage their estates after death. This has insured that the gifts left will be used for the purposes that the giver intended.

My wife worked a number of years for a large university. She was in charge of the Development Board. These volunteers' primary responsibility was to raise money for the university. A giver had many choices as to where their gifts could be spent. It was most often to sponsor scholarships, build buildings or be left to the discretion of the university to be used as they saw fit. Often, industry or governmental entities would match contributions.

As a community volunteer, I have raised many dollars. One of the best sales points was simply the tax implications. Most people would rather give to almost any worthwhile cause rather than the government. However, a true philanthropist gives to help those in need.

The greatest gift that anyone could give is their life. Many men and women have done so to protect our freedom. Can you put a price on just one life?

CHAPTER 42

INCORRIGIBLE

I REMEMBER AN OLDER lady making a remark about my twin brother that I just didn't understand. We were horsing around at my grandmother's house on a Sunday afternoon. Joe made some comment and she stated that he was incorrigible. What did that mean? Throughout my life, I have heard the statement only a few times. Therefore, I thought that it was time to refer to Webster's Dictionary to learn its' meaning.

It means... Beyond correction or reform. One who cannot be reformed. Well based on my teachings. All of us can change. However, if we continue bad habits or at least project an attitude of not wanting to become a better person: then perhaps we could be labeled as being incorrigible. I am sure that at different stages of my life; those around me put me in such a category.

Perhaps a stubborn attitude or resenting change could be perceived as such characteristic. Often, we project such tendencies without evening knowing it. Think about people that you have known that it seemed everything they did was wrong or evil. Do you think it was premeditated? I think probably not. The old saying: "If she didn't have bad luck, she would have no luck at all", seems to come into play.

If you take time to study such persons, you would learn that they have had little or no coaching or positive reinforcement that creates an eager want to be positive. It is sad. However, many children in today's society are living without parents and are homeless. Just how do they learn not to be incorrigible? When you are hungry or have no place to call home, you become very defensive and will turn to unthinkable actives just to survive. Perhaps, we cause some people to become incorrigible due to our lack of understanding their circumstances or our failure to help them to do better. By not criticizing or complaining, but rather offering the appropriate positive reinforcement; we may provide the path for new thinking that will change the person.

The next time that you identify a person as being incorrigible, stop and try to determine what has made them to act in such a fashion? Also, we need to look at ourselves. Do we appear to be incorrigible to others? We need to think before we act and always strive to do what we know is right and ethical.

CHAPTER 43

HYPOCHONDRIAC

WHILE GROWING UP in rural South Alabama you often heard grown-ups greet each other by asking, "How are you"? Depending on who was asked, would dictate the amount of time that you would spend getting the response. Most of the time a simple "just fine" or "O.K." would be the answer. However, sometimes you would learn far more than you wanted to know about the wellbeing of the person that you asked. It might lead to a full health report on other relatives.

We have family members that live to go to the doctor. Often, they have multiple appointments schedule. They take the time to research their ailment, so they will be prepared to make their own diagnostics and argue with the doctor about their findings. Every prescription that is suggested is the wrong one. While it may help in one are, it does more damage to other parts of the body.

Hypochondriacs are never well. They have so many imaginary ailments that when a real one comes about, they cannot recognize it. Mother would tell us that we had better not complain about being sick to stay home from school on a test day because the good Lord would make us ill for lying.

I have read where people almost bankrupt families by habitual visits to doctors just to gain personal attention. Some less than honest doctors make a lot of money via such visits. Unnecessary treatments can lead to a very dangerous outcome. Some folks have selective surgery for the purpose of satisfying the need to bring attention to themselves. These could lead to a much worse situation, including disfigurement or even death.

As we grow older, we have aches and pains that we didn't' experience at a younger age. However, these do not necessarily dictate that we have a physical problem. We should exercise, eat properly, and get plenty of sleep to stay healthy. Annual check-ups and following our doctors' instructions will give us longer and happier lives.

Do you complain about your health when you should be counting your blessings?

CHAPTER 44

INDECISIVE

D O YOU KNOW someone that has a hard time making a decision? It could be as simple as to what clothes to wear or where to sit at a public function. We are all faced with hundreds of decisions daily. Most are not major but run of the mill daily activities.

Once, I had a boss that wanted to review every piece of correspondence that was prepared by any member of his team before it was sent. He would labor over a single word and often make changes to the second or third revision. Not only did his indecisiveness cost him lots of time but it was a demoralizing to his team.

Just imagine a doctor in the operating room not having the ability to make quick decisions. The same is true with all first responders, race car drivers, military personal involved in battle and parents raising children. These situations require immediate decisions to protect property and lives.

There are many times that we need to review all the information available to us before making a major decision. Some examples would be buying a new home, car, or other expensive items. Most of the time, we would get a second opinion before having surgery or health related procedures.

Some of the decisions that we make are binding and obligate us beyond what we may have been thinking at the moment the decision was made. An example would be picking a mate to marry or deciding to have children. Also, picking a career or agreeing to accept a job will extend our commitment into the future. Can you think of others? Have you ever made decisions that obligated you into the future which you would do differently if given the opportunity to do it over?

It is most important that we balance the quality of our decisions with timeliness of the same. On occasion it is better to make a fair decision in a timely manner than to procrastinate trying to learn every small detail which would not have much of an impact anyway. We are all different and our brains function differently, just remember there are many answers to the same question and they are all correct.

SUMMARY

LET'S TAKE A few minutes to identify some of our own personality traits. First, list seven traits that were included in this book that you consider to be positive. Next, place a star next to each one that you possess. Now, rate yourself as to your strength in these categories, with 1 being the lowest and 5 the highest. Perhaps you can list some traits that were not included in the book. These are equally important. What is your plan to improve in the areas where you scored 3 or less?

Next, list at least five traits that you feel were negative. Do you possess any of these? If so, what is your plan to change? Make a follow-up for six months from today to review the results of your self-help strategy. If you know that you have improved in half of more of your own personality traits, you should treat yourself to something special to celebrate.

This process should be repeated annually. We should never stop trying to improve ourselves. I am proud of you!

Printed in the United States
By Bookmasters